LEGENDS
of the
SUN and MOON

by Eric and Tessa Hadley

illustrated by Jan Nesbitt

CAMBRIDGE UNIVERSITY PRESS

Cambridge
London   New York   New Rochelle
Melbourne   Sydney

Other legends books from Cambridge

Legends of Earth, Air, Fire and Water by Eric and Tessa Hadley

Legends of the Animal World by Rosalind Kerven

The Shining Stars by Ghislaine Vautier and Kenneth McLeish

The Way of the Stars by Ghislaine Vautier and Kenneth McLeish

The Seven Wonders of the World by Kenneth McLeish

Published by the Press Syndicate of the University of Cambridge
The Pitt Building, Trumpington Street, Cambridge CB2 1RP
32 East 57th Street, New York, NY 10022, USA
10 Stamford Road, Oakleigh, Melbourne 3166, Australia

First published 1983
Reprinted 1986

Printed in Hong Kong

Library of Congress catalogue card number: 82–17720

British Library cataloguing in publication data
Hadley, Eric
Legends of the sun and moon.
1. Sun – Folklore – Juvenile literature
2. Moon – Folklore – Juvenile literature
I. Title   II. Hadley, Tessa
III. Nesbitt, Jan
398.2'6   PZ10.3

ISBN 0 521 25227 X

CONTENTS

ABOUT THE STORIES

The stories in this collection were told long ago by people from many different lands and cultures. They were important to them in ways which we may find difficult to understand. They were so important that they were told over and over again, and so powerful in one case – the story of Anansi and his six sons – that the story survived even when the people who told it had been shipped as slaves from one continent to another, from West Africa to the islands of the West Indies. In a foreign country and robbed of their freedom, they were still *a people* as long as they could go on telling the stories they had brought with them.

Some of the stories people told were stories about the Sun and Moon. It's hardly surprising: the light from the Sun woke them each day. Hunting in desert and forest, fishing at sea or working on their crops, they felt its heat. The Sun's heat could scorch and burn, but without it nothing would grow and everyone would go hungry. And there were other times when they could rest or play in its warmth.

In the evenings, they came together to tell their tales in the light of the Moon, or to fill the darkness when the Moon mysteriously grew thin and disappeared. The evening is the time for telling the stories that bind a people together.

Today, we know things about the Sun and Moon that these people didn't: we know that the Sun is a fiery ball of glowing gas, and we know that the Moon is a lump of barren rock. Men have been to the Moon and left their footprints. We think that gives us all the answers. But the storytellers were interested in explaining things too. They were interested in how the Sun and Moon came to be where they are, how they moved across the sky and where they went when they disappeared. The stories are full of their thoughts about these things.

But there is a difference between us and these storytellers. They felt directly the power of the Sun and Moon in their lives. The Sun and the Moon in their stories are as attractive, difficult and changeable as people. They can be frightening, they can be angry or jealous, or they can bring hope and happiness. Sometimes the Sun and the Moon seem very human – they share our cleverness and our stupidity, our sense of fun and our seriousness. At other times their power and mystery is beyond what a human being can do or know. But always the stories speak of the Sun and Moon as part of the lives of men, women and children. They don't banish them millions of miles into space to be forgotten or finished with. Each new story is a new place to begin wondering from . . . and that is a good place to begin.

Where the stories come from

NORTH
AMERICA

(Blackfoot
Indians)

(Cherokee
Indians)

MEXICO

ARMENIA

INDIA

NIGERIA

POLYNESIA

AUSTRALIA
(Aborigines)

NEW ZEALAND
(Maoris)

THE BONFIRE

Creating the world took time, you know. And Baiame the Great Spirit sometimes made mistakes. The first birds and animals he made, for instance, grew and grew to an enormous size, and then there wasn't enough for them to eat, so they fought each other. They fought in the dark. Baiame hadn't made light yet: there was only the dim light of the stars.

This all made the earth a very uncomfortable place, so Baiame and Punjel lived in the Milky Way, where it was cold, cold, cold, far out in space. Every day the gods collected firewood for a great bonfire.

"Brrrrr," shivered Punjel. "Haven't we got enough yet? When do we set fire to this lot?"

"We don't," said Baiame. "We haven't got fire yet."

"Haven't got it? Well why don't we go and get it? I'm freezing!"

"Don't hurry me," said Baiame. "Everything in its own good time."

"It's all very well …"

Wheeeeeeeeee! A great white egg came hurtling through space. Punjel put out his hand to catch it, but it slipped through his fingers and smashed.

"Oh! Look at this mess!" said Punjel.

There was egg over everything. Yellow egg and clear egg all over their lovely bonfire.

Whoosh! The wonderful egg burst into flame!

Crackle! The tinder-dry wood blazed up in no time!

"Hurrah!" shouted Punjel. "Fire! I'm warm at last!"

"Didn't I tell you?" said Baiame.

The gods toasted themselves in front of the bonfire that blazed higher and higher, yellow and red and blue and orange. It made more light than the dim light of the stars. It made so much light that when the gods looked down, they could see the whole world for the first time.

The gold light on the mountain tops!

The green leaves of the trees dancing in the wind!

The tall grey waves of the sea!

The silver sparkling of the streams and waterfalls!

The yellow sands of the desert!

The clouds that spread their shade!

"So this is what you have been up to in the dark!" said Punjel. "It's beautiful! Is it for us?"

"Not only for us." said Baiame. "I want to make some new creatures to live in it. I've had enough of those birds and animals that have grown too big. They were all very well for the dark: now I'm planning something much more delicate and complicated:

Silvery fishes to fill the lakes and rivers!

Insects small as grains of sand!

Red birds to hum among the flowers!

Snakes that slip out of their skins!

Scampering mice!

I've no end of ideas!"

"The fire's going out," cried Punjel. "What shall we do? All your ideas will get us nowhere if we can't see!"

"It's alright," said Baiame. "I'll light it again in the morning. When I make men they'll call it Sun. The fire will go out every night, and I'll light another one every morning. Men will know that when Sun comes, it is time to wake up out of their sleep."

"What is sleep?" asked Punjel.

"It is like death, but not death," explained Baiame. "Men need to rest from living. It tires them out."

"How odd," said Punjel.

Aboriginal

At last, these words rose above the argument:

"No more. There must be an end to this."

Two gods spoke and stepped forward to offer themselves to give light to the world. One was rich and strong and the other was poor and feeble.

"As the sun I shall be even richer and stronger," said Rich and Strong.

"As the sun I shall give warmth and light to the world," said Poor and Feeble.

Even Quezalcoatl agreed. When he had been the second sun he had left every living plant uprooted by the mighty hurricane that blew as he fell from sky to earth. And Tezcatlipoca, the Black God, the first sun, brooded silent in the darkness with which he had

There have been other suns – four in all – but this is the story of our sun: the fifth and final sun.

First, there had been Tezcatlipoca, torn from the sky by Quezalcoatl.

Quezalcoatl had been second sun, but he was hurled into the sea by Tezcatlipoca.

First sun, second sun, third sun, fourth sun: all had failed. So the gods agreed to meet together.

"There must be a sun to light the earth by day."

"There must be a moon to light the earth by night."

They spoke these words with one voice but then they argued for four days about who amongst them should become sun and moon.

INAL SUN

surrounded the arguing gods.

The darkness disappeared when the gods built a great bonfire whose flames leaped into the sky.

Rich and Strong approached the fire and stared into the flaming logs and embers. Three times he drew near, three times he drew back. He feared the flames.

Poor and Feeble approached the fire, stared into the flaming logs and embers … and leapt! … Aieeeee! … A vast flame sprang upwards like a huge arrow of fire and where the arrow tip reached the sky, the sun appeared … the fifth and final sun.

There was a great roar of pleasure from the gods: no-one roared louder than Quezalcoatl. Even Tezcatlipoca, the Black God, was satisfied. The night still belonged to him.

One god remained silent. Rich and strong he was, but not strong enough to be the sun. He drew near to the fire, and, no drawing back this time, he flung himself into the flames. But the flames were dying and the embers had lost their great heat. No arrow of flame came springing forth. Slowly, from the ashes, the moon sailed into the sky, the feeble follower of the sun.

This time the gods shouted with anger. All, that is, except Tezcatlipoca, the Black God. Now he had more than the evening star to light the spots on his tiger coat in the hours of blackness.

Mexican

OLD MAN AND THE SUN

Old Man was travelling about, making things as he went; putting rivers here and there, making birds and animals as he passed along, making people by working the clay and blowing his breath into it.

Old Man travelled until he came to the Sun's lodge. The Sun asked him to stay awhile and Old Man was very glad to do so.

He stayed until the meat ran out and the Sun said,

"Old Man, shall we go and kill some deer?"

"Agreed," said the Old Man, "I like deer meat."

Old Man looked on as the Sun took down a bag and pulled from it a pair of leggings embroidered with porcupine quills and bright feathers.

"These are my hunting leggings," said the Sun, "and they have great power. If I put them on and walk around a patch of brush, it bursts into flames, the deer run out, and I shoot them with my arrows."

"Wonderful," Old Man exclaimed, and he thought to himself, "I must have those leggings, even if I have to steal them."

During the hunt, the leggings worked just as the Sun had said they would.

During the night, Old Man stole them from where they lay at the Sun's side, just as he'd promised himself he would.

Old Man travelled a long time, until sleep overcame him. Then he lay down and slept, using the leggings as a pillow. He was woken up by a voice which said:

"Old Man, why are my leggings under your head?"

Old Man was puzzled. It was the Sun's voice and he was still in the Sun's lodge. "I must have wandered round in a circle," he thought.

"Oh, I couldn't find anything for a pillow, so I just put these under my head," he lied.

The next night, it was the same story. Old Man stole the leggings and ran off. He kept running until just before morning, and then lay down and slept. You see what a fool he was. He did not know that the whole world is the Sun's lodge. He did not know that no matter how far he ran, he could never escape from the Sun's sight or his voice.

"Old Man, I see you like my leggings. Keep them. I will give them to you."

Old Man travelled on, feeling very pleased with himself, but he was hungry and he had no meat. He pulled on his leggings and a patch of brush nearby burst into flames. Out ran the deer, rushing towards him: but so did the fire. Old Man dropped his bow and ran, but the fire gained on him and began to burn his legs. His leggings were all on fire. He came to a river and jumped in, ripping off the leggings. But they were burned to pieces.

"That'll teach you a lesson." It was Sun's voice again.

But Old Man pretended not to hear. He pulled himself out of the river and was off on his travels again, looking for something new.

Blackfoot Indian

SUN, MOON
AND WATER

Long ago, before humans first walked on the earth, the Sun and Moon lived together in Africa as man and wife.

The Sun's greatest friend was the Water, and he said to Water one day:

"Here I am, visiting you again and yet not once have you ever visited me."

"Ah," gurgled the Water, "I should love to visit you and to meet your lovely wife the Moon. But I'm afraid your house is too small for me and all those who come with me, as part of me, wherever I flow.

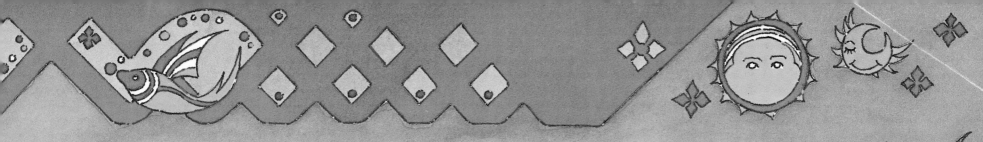

You know, the shellfish, the starfish and butterfly fish, the shoals of sardines and swarms of mackerel, the sharp-toothed shark and the mighty whale. Build yourself a huge kraal and I will visit you with pleasure, again and again."

"That's just what I'll do," said the Sun. And he set to work immediately and built a great collection of huts surrounded by a fence, a kraal, that stretched out in all directions as far as the eye could see.

When the vast kraal was completed, the Sun sent his invitation to the Water. Soon he and his wife, the Moon, could see the Water coming. Miles away they could see him flowing in across the plains, making his way amongst the trees and hills until, at last, he swirled in about their ankles.

"Here I am, dear Sun, so pleased to be here and to be meeting your wife. What a big and beautiful place you've built for me to visit you."

Even as he spoke the Sun and Moon were knee-deep in the Water sparkling with fishes big and small.

"Are you sure you've got room for us all?" bubbled the Water. "We're not all here yet."

"Certainly," smiled the Sun.

"Without a doubt," beamed the Moon.

But as they said this Sun and Moon perched on the highest part of their roof while the flying fishes flashed past them in the air.

"Are you sure you've got room for us all?" gargled the Water, his voice almost lost as the whales crashed and blew.

He could not have heard the Moon as she whispered fearfully, "I believe you're filling our kraal to overflowing."

Nonsense," shouted the Sun. "There's room for everyone."

But there wasn't. The Water was already lapping over the top of the roof and, to escape, the Sun and the Moon had to make a mighty leap high into the sky. Their leap carried them so far that from the earth the Sun looked no bigger than a small plum. And as they leapt up, the Moon said to the Sun, "I told you he was filling our kraal to overflowing!"

These were the last sad words the Moon ever spoke on earth.

Nigerian

THE SUN'S DAUGHTER

Sun and Moon were talking.
"Aren't men and women ugly?" said Sun. "They look up at me with such funny screwed up faces, poor things."

Moon smiled at her in surprise.

"Men and women? I think they're very pretty!" he said. "Those soft silvery faces! And such sweet smiles when they look up at me!"

Now Sun looked surprised: and it didn't take her long to feel jealous.

"Well, if they won't smile at me, I'll burn them up," she thought. Now, every day at noon she visited her daughter's house in the highest part of the sky. And there she burned with such fierce heat she parched the earth and started a fever among the people.

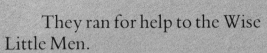

They ran for help to the Wise Little Men.

"Little Men, Little Men, what can we do? Our parents and our children and our friends are all dead, and we will die too, if you don't help us destroy the Sun."

The Wise Little Men shook their heads.

"You want to destroy the Sun? Well, put the rattlesnake where he can bite her tomorrow when she visits her daughter's house."

But the rattlesnake was too quick. When the Sun's daughter flew to her door to welcome her mother he bit her instead, on the forehead, and she died. And the Sun sank down into a dark place to mourn for her lost child.

"Little Men, Little Men, what can we do? We are in the dark, day and night, and nothing will grow, and we can't keep warm. We will die, if you don't help us to bring back the Sun."

"You want to bring back the Sun?

Well, you had better fetch her daughter back from the Ghosts in the Darkening Land. Take a box to put her in: but whatever you do don't open the box before you get her home."

They went to the Darkening Land, and found the Sun's daughter dancing with the other Ghosts. They caught tight hold of her, tucked her in the box, and started home.

"Let me out, let me out, I am so thirsty!" she cried, but they took no notice.

"Let me out, let me out, I am so hungry!" she cried, but they took no notice.

"Let me out, let me out, I can't breathe!" she cried when they were nearly there: and they opened the box just a very little to give her some air.

Whoosh! Something flew past them into the trees, and there was a redbird singing on a branch.

When the Sun knew that her daughter had turned into a redbird, she began to cry, and she cried so long there was a flood on the earth.

"Little Men, Little Men, what can we do? The whole world will be drowned, and we will die too, if you don't help us make the Sun smile again."

"You want to make the Sun smile? Well, you'd better send some of your best-looking young people to sing and dance for her."

At first the Sun wouldn't look. But nobody can shut their ears to music, however sad they are. When the drummer changed the song, the Sun lifted her head. And when she saw how beautiful they were, she smiled, and stopped her crying.

Cherokee Indian

THE FAT MOON

Bahloo the Moon grew fat. At night when he kissed the earth with his silver light, men looked up and smiled at him, but they never thought he might be lonely.

Bahloo loved girls. He loved them brown-skinned and plump with teasing black eyes and black hair pushed behind their ears. And he longed for one to cuddle and keep him happy in the empty sky.

When the campfires were burning and the girls were dancing round, Bahloo came down close to the earth and bent his shining head to speak to them. But the girls laughed and scampered off. They didn't like

him, fat white thing, with his arms and legs like twigs.

One night two girls were sitting chattering on the riverbank.

"How beautiful the moonlight is," sighed one.

Now, Bahloo just happened to be passing. When he saw the girls he broke into a run, puffing and blowing, his big belly shaking. The girls were so surprised, they didn't know whether to laugh or shout for help: they ran off and stood gazing at him from a safe distance.

Bahloo sat down at the side of the river and big silver teardrops rolled out of his eyes and down his round white face.

"Little flowers," he wept, "why do you hate me? I spend night after night so far from the campfires and the fun. All I want is a bit of company."

The girls felt sorry for Bahloo.

One of them sang him a song.

One of them danced him a dance.

"Now, just take me over to the other side, my loves, in your canoe, then you must go home to your beds, and I'll go to mine."

When Bahloo was sat in the canoe, holding on tight to the sides with his twiggy arms, there was no room for anyone else. So the girls swam one on either side, pushing him between them. The moonlight shone on the river, and on the twinkling arms and legs of the girls as they swam, and their hair streamed out behind them.

Mmmmmmm! Bahloo reached out one hand to touch one of them ever so lightly.

"Bahloo! Keep still," she said.

But Bahloo couldn't help it.

"Bahloo! Don't tickle!" said the other one.

But Bahloo was shining very bright indeed, and he tried to grab tight hold of one of the girls.

"Bahloo! Let go of us, or we'll scream!"

"Scream all you like," said Bahloo, "no-one will hear."

And he bent down his shining head for a kiss.

But then one girl pushed and one girl pulled and …

Splash!

The round shining moon sank down, down into the water, and his light grew fainter and fainter, until they could just see a pale silver blur at the bottom of the river.

"Oh!" cried the girls. "What have we done?"

And they ran home to tell the old ones.

"The nights will be dark again, and long, without that silver moon to cheer us up," the old ones complained, huddling closer round the fire.

"Oh, he'll be back, don't worry," said Wahn the wise crow. "But he's rather ashamed of himself. Look: there he is, trying to climb into the sky without anybody noticing."

And so he was. But poor Bahloo was only poor *thin* Bahloo now, only a pale sliver of a Moon.

"He'll grow," said Wahn. "He'll get just as fat as ever he was – and just as wicked – until the next time someone teaches him a lesson."

Aboriginal

THE YOUNG HUNTER

For three days the young hunter had not caught anything. He was an idle, good-natured young man: but this evening his feet were sore, he was hungry and thirsty, and his game-bag was empty. He kicked his way through a little wood, grumbling to himself.

"And you!" he glowered at the low, pale evening Sun. "You scorch me, you parch me, you make me sweat, you shine in my eyes when I take aim … I've a good mind to …".

He lifted up his bow and squinted at the Sun along his arrow.

"A nice sitting target! I'll put you out, and we'll live by candlelight instead, eh?"

Suddenly a mighty blow from an invisible fist knocked the solid earth from under him and he sprawled on the path. Hot breath scorched his eyebrows.

"Miserable mortal! Don't trifle with me," exclaimed the Sun. "You'll pay for your cheek! Step into my light ever again, and you'll die: I'll put *you* out!"

The young man lay still for a long time; when he lifted his head the Sun had gone and it was night. He crawled to a deep cave and hid himself. Days passed: he didn't dare go out in them; by night he stumbled after whatever food he could find. He lived like a mole under the Sun's curse. But he dreamed all the time of his wife and baby, and one night he found himself on the familiar way home.

"I don't care about the curse," he said, and he walked boldly into the town, and knocked on the window of his parents' house. His wife ran to let him in; mother, father, wife, they kissed him, pressed his hands to their cheeks. For the first time for a long time he drank wine and ate hot food. Life was good.

But when morning light came the young man fell on his bed and lay still like death.

His mother put on her iron shoes and walked west to the ends of the earth. There stood a splendid palace of blue marble. She went in at the gate, and through the first twelve courts, where the stars lay sleeping. In the last court was a beautiful woman on a bed of pearls. She was the Sun's mother.

"Dear lady," said the old woman, "forgive me for disturbing you here. But listen to my son's story, and the foolish thing he said in a bad temper."

The Sun's mother listened.

"Yes," she sighed, "my son has a temper too. But I think I can help you. Tonight when my son has washed himself, steal a little water from his bath and take it home to your son. Now hide yourself, old woman, for he's on his way, and I don't want you burnt to death."

The old woman hid.

In strode the Sun, crimson and trailing clouds from the sunset. He splashed hissing and steaming into a crystal pool. Then when he was clear and yellow again he curled up like a little child at his mother's breast to suck her milk, to give him strength to be new born next morning.

The old woman stole a little water from his bath.

At home her son still lay like death on his bed. But when she sprinkled him with the Sun's bathwater he got up as strong as he ever had been and stronger! And for seven days and nights they feasted and danced and sang, and the young hunter strolled cheerfully among his guests in the bright sunshine.

Armenian

MAUI SLOWS DOWN THE SUN

Maui the trickster felt bothered. He felt as though he was always in a hurry.

"One minute the Sun rises, next minute down it goes, and it's time for bed! I never get anything finished – and look at the poor fishermen and the women, trying to keep up with all their work! I've had enough of that lazy Sun! Time there was a change!"

Maui had a think. To make the Sun slow down they had better catch him first.

They tried three times.

First, they tried rope made of coconut fibre. Maui and his brothers plaited it. Then they dragged it out to the horizon, tied it in a noose, and laid it round the edge of the pit where the Sun hides at night. They crouched down to wait.

Wham! Out flew the Sun, and the rope snapped like a strand of cobweb.

"Mmm. I thought that would happen," said Maui. "Luckily, I've got another plan."

The second time, they tried more coconut rope: a rope as thick as a tree, plaited out of all the coconuts in the island.

Wham! Out flew the Sun, the noose tightened, Maui and his brothers held on like madmen, the Sun shuddered and strained for a moment … but the ropes shrivelled in the heat. The Sun shot on across the sky; Maui and his brothers fell in a heap.

"Hmmm. I had a feeling we were wrong sticking to coconut rope. Luckily I've got a better idea."

The third time, Maui needed his sister, Hina, to help. She cut off all her magic hair for him.

"This should do the trick!" said Maui, plaiting busily.

They put the noose around the pit, and lay in wait for the dawn.

Wham! Out flew the Sun, the noose tightened, Maui and his brothers held on like demons, the Sun shuddered and strained and struggled and twisted about and screamed …

"Listen to me!" shouted Maui. "I'll let you go – if you promise to slow down, and give us more hours in the day."

The Sun wriggled and writhed, and the sweat flew off Maui and his brothers, but they held on.

"Aaagh! I will! I promise!" yelled the Sun at last.

Maui and his brothers let go, and fell in a heap.

Up soared the Sun into the morning sky.

"I told you it would work!" said Maui.

"We'd better go off fishing before it gets dark," said the others.

"There's no hurry," said Maui. "We've got plenty of time now. Sit down, take a rest."

But the others couldn't get used to it and off they went. Maui stretched out on a sandbank, and lay thinking happily all the long long day. And when the Sun did set at last, there were the hair ropes, still trailing from it into the sea!

"How pretty!" thought Maui. "How nice to have time to notice."

Maori

THE WOMAN IN THE MOON

You've heard of the man in the Moon? Well, is it a man? Listen, and look hard next time.

There was once a woman called Rona whose husband was a fisherman.

"Wife," he said one day, "tonight is a good night for fishing. We'll have bright moonlight. I'll take the boys with me to the offshore island where I know there are plenty of fish. We'll be back with full nets tomorrow night. See that you have a good meal waiting for us."

That was how he always said it, just like that. Rona said nothing.

The next night, as the shadows lengthened, Rona began to prepare the meal. She worked quickly and without fuss. Every part of the job and its precise order were so well known to her. By the time she heard the song of the returning fishermen the heated stones of the oven glowed red in the dusk and leaves lay ready to cover the food while it cooked. But in the moment of placing the food in her oven and covering it she realised that she had no water to sprinkle over the hot stones to make them steam.

Snatching up two calabashes she ran down the path to the spring. The silver light of the full moon lit up the track clearly in front of her as she raced along. That is, until a passing cloud cut off the light. She rushed on blind through the blackness and stubbed her toe on a tree root, then she stumbled into a rock, scraping her shin.

The pain pushed a great cry out of her.

"Pokokohua! Cooked head!" she screamed. "Curse you Moon, for putting out your light."

The Moon heard her cry and coming down from the sky it caught Rona in its hands and began to carry her away. Rona grasped the branch of a tree and held on with all her strength. The Moon tugged harder and, you know, no-one can match the power of a god. But Rona did.

There was the sound of cracking and splintering as the tree's roots were torn from the ground and it was carried, along with Rona, far into the sky.

The tune of the fisherman and his sons soon changed when they found the uncooked food on the cold stones, and no sign of Rona. Finally, as they looked about them, they lifted their eyes up to the night sky and saw Rona on the face of the full Moon, sitting there glumly, but still clutching the uprooted tree and her calabashes.

They remembered Rona, and don't you forget her.

Maori

THE DISOBEDIENT SUN-CHILD

In a house by the sea, behind a high fence, there lived a mother and her little boy. He was a beautiful little boy, shining like the sun. They kept themselves to themselves: the boy didn't play much with the other children.

"Yah! Who's your father then? Don't you even know?" they teased him.

"Not common like yours!" he shouted back. But he ran home angry to his mother.

"Well? Who *is* my father then?"

Thoughtfully she stirred the pot.

"Years ago," she said, "I was so beautiful that my father was afraid of what might become of me. So he shut me up here, behind the high fence, away from men. But no high fence could stop your father."

"Well, who is he?"

"He watched me all day, and at night he hid his brightness under a cloak, and visited me. Then you were born."

"But who *is* he?" The boy stamped his foot. "Tell me!"

"The Sun himself, of course."

"Of course!" said the boy in amazement. He couldn't help boasting to the others.

"My father is a prince and lives in the sky!"

"Oh yes? Mine's a fish and he lives up a tree!"

"If he's a prince, why haven't you got a new shirt?"

They strutted off holding their noses, then fell about with laughter.

When the sun-child grew to be a man, he set off in a canoe to find his father.

"Tell him I don't forget him," said his mother.

The sun-child paddled and paddled to the place where the Sun rises. It grew dark and the stars came out. Strange sea-creatures swam

alongside him, and gazed at him with eyes like lamps.

"Father!" he shouted at last.

The red tip of the Sun showed above the horizon, and a great roar made the sea tremble.

"Who dares to call me father?"

"I am your son from Tongatabu, and I have come to live with you."

"Go home boy. I've no time to spare: I have to light up all the islands in the ocean! Go home to your own good people."

"Father! I'm not like them! Let me stay!"

"No," said the Sun, and he slid a little further over the horizon, changing the dark sea to dancing colours. "But listen, boy. In the Moon there are two shells, Monuia and Melaia. Beware Monuia. Take Melaia as a gift from me. It will make you a leader among men."

And the Sun sailed up into the sky, and the day began. All that long day the sun-child brooded in his canoe. When night came, instead of stealing Melaia as his father had told him to do, he stole Monuia out of the Moon.

"Perhaps this one will make me more than a leader among men. Perhaps it will make me a god like my father!"

He stood in his canoe, and held the curved pink shell up high in the moonlight. From all the corners of the sea the fish came swimming towards Monuia. Whales and dolphins, sharks and swordfish; big, little, silver, rainbow-coloured, fat and flat fish; nearer and nearer they came.

"Look! I am a god! The fish are coming to do me honour!"

The water frothed and foamed, the fish leaped up towards the glowing shell, and in the confusion the canoe was overturned, and the proud sun-child sank deep into the dark water and drowned. Ah! If only he'd taken his father's gift, who knows what he might have become?

Polynesian

ANANSI'S SIX SONS

Spider Anansi had six skilful sons. One day he went on a long journey leaving his six sons behind. The weeks passed, but Anansi didn't return, and his sons began to worry.

Akakai, the first son, climbed a high mountain to look for his father. His sight was so sharp he could see trouble coming for miles off. Soon he called down to his brothers:

"Our father needs our help. He has fallen into a deep river, but to get to it we have to make our way through the thickest jungle I've ever seen."

"Leave it to me," cried Twa Akwan. In no time he had cut a path straight through that jungle and the brothers swept along it to the edge of the river.

While the rest of them paused, wondering what to do next, Hwe Nsuo bent down to take a drink from the river. When he stood up to wipe his face the river bed was dry and a great fish lay gasping and flapping at their feet.

In one movement Adwafo leapt on the fish and slit it open. Out stepped Anansi.

But they had no sooner clambered back safely to the river bank than a huge hawk swooped out of the sky, caught Anansi in his beak and soared into the air with him. Toto Abuo picked up a rock and hurled it after them: it struck the hawk and made him drop Anansi. And as he did so, the sixth son, Da Yi Ya, threw himself on the ground like a cushion and softened his father's fall.

Anansi was pleased with his sons but he could not think of how to reward them. Then one day walking through the forest he came upon a beautiful bright light shining steadily in the gloom. This was no flickering fire-light: it was so lovely that he decided to give it to one of his sons.

To help him decide which one to give it to he called upon Nyame, the Sky God, and soon they were all gathered together: Anansi, his six sons, and Nyame, who held the beautiful light.

When they saw it they all wanted it, and very soon what had begun as an argument had become an ugly fight.

At last, Nyame stood up and silenced them.

"This light that Anansi has found is very beautiful. But before it came you lived peacefully together. Now I hear nothing but hard words and hard blows. You want it Akakai, and you Twa Akwan, and you, and you …"

And taking the light, Nyame hurled it into the sky – higher it soared even than Toto Abuo's rock. And there the Moon stayed, not on the earth where Anansi found it, but beyond the reach even of his skilful sons.

West African and Haitian

THE HARES AND THE ELEPHANTS

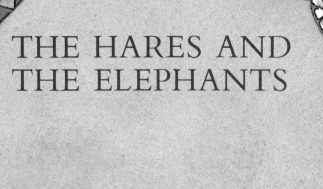

There was a drought – the rains had failed – and the elephants stood miserably round their dwindling water-hole. They longed for a pool of clear water where they could drink their fill and cool their skins.

The leader of the herd set off in search of such a pool and he found the very thing not far off. It was a lake, cool and deep, and all was well again for the elephants.

But the hares who lived by the lake found the elephants very unwelcome visitors. When they gathered together their leader spoke for all of them:

"It's all very well for these elephants, but we shall all be crushed under their trampling feet."

It was an old and wise hare who offered to put a stop to it. Off he went to the elephants, but as he went he thought to himself:

"What am I going to say? How do you address an elephant? He could kill me with a mere touch."

There was a mound near the lake. The hare climbed to the top of it and called out to the elephant leader:

"Mighty elephant, listen to me!"

"Where have you popped up from?"

"I am an ambassador from his worship the Moon."

"State your business," said the elephant respectfully.

"I have been commanded by the Moon to give you this message. Listen, this is what he has said. 'Why have you trampled and scattered my hares? Don't you understand that they are my subjects and that they guard my Moonlake?'"

The leader of the herd was terrified:

"We didn't know. We won't go there again."

"Words are not enough," said the hare. "Come to the lake with me tonight."

That night, the night of the full Moon, they both stood at the lakeside.

"Now, elephant," the hare commanded, "bow down before the Moon, who is trembling in anger in the lake there. Beg his forgiveness and go."

The elephant sank to his knees, hardly daring to look at the rippling reflection of the Moon in the waters.

"Great lord Moon," the hare continued, "forgive this poor creature. He is ignorant." And then he sent the elephant packing.

The hares lived in peace again. Now, could that just be the shape of a hare in the Moon?

Indian

MORE ABOUT THE SUN AND MOON

Does the Sun go round the Earth or does the Earth go round the Sun? That may seem a simple question – of course, the Earth goes round the Sun. But if someone asks you how you *know* the Earth goes round the Sun, the answer is much more difficult. You can't say, "It's obvious, just go and look." As far as we can *see*, the Earth does not move, and every day the Sun seems to move across the sky from east to west. We talk as if the Sun moves; we say it *comes up* in the morning and *goes down* at night.

So to say that the Earth moves we have to learn *not* to believe what we see. It is very hard to make anyone do that. What we usually say to prove something really happened is, "I saw it with my own eyes." But much of what we know today about how the Sun, Moon and Earth move comes from men who said, "We *don't* trust what we see. Things may look like this from where we stand on Earth, but they might look very different from somewhere else."

The first people not to trust what they saw were the Greek scientists who lived five or six centuries before the birth of Christ. They were interested in the changes they saw in the movements of the planets and the stars. In fact, our word

"planet" comes from a Greek word meaning "wanderer". When they tried to explain these movements they usually stuck with the idea that the Earth stood still while the Sun, Moon and planets moved around it. Then, in the third century B.C., an astronomer called Aristarchus thought that we could also explain these movements by imagining that the Earth and all the other planets moved round the Sun. More than that, he explained the daily rising and setting of the Sun by suggesting that on its yearly

The Ancient Greek view of the Universe with the Earth at the centre.

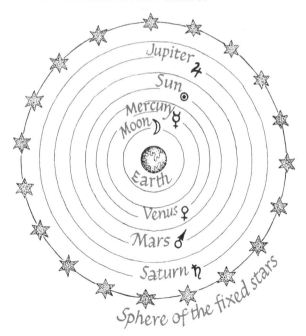

journey round the Sun, the Earth turned round once a day.

Aristarchus' theory was never seriously accepted. Then, for a long time, the knowledge and ideas of the Greeks were lost and it was to be eighteen hundred years before anyone else returned to them. The thought of a moving spinning Earth was much less comfortable than the idea most people then believed in, of an Earth firmly fixed, with the Sun, Moon and planets moving round it. The feeling of being fixed and closed in was very satisfying, like being tucked up warmly in bed at night.

But there are always people who are more adventurous than that. Christopher Columbus the great explorer is a good example. Columbus sailed west into the Atlantic Ocean to find a new route to Asia, but instead he found a new continent, America. He changed the map of the world, and so changed everyone's mind about what the Earth was like.

Not long after Columbus' great discoveries the safe map of the Universe was changed by a Polish astronomer called Nicholas Copernicus, born in 1473. What Copernicus and the astronomers who followed him did was to say again, "We don't trust what we see." In other

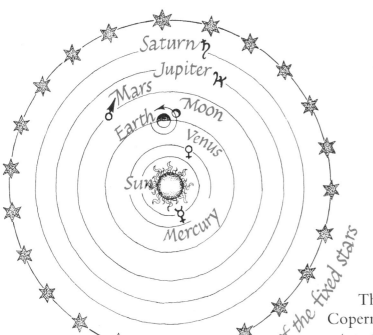

Copernicus's view of the Universe with the Sun at the centre.

Kepler proved that the path of the planets round the Sun is elliptical. This diagram shows how to draw an ellipse.

words, Copernicus changed his point of view; it is as if he stopped looking at the Universe from the Earth, and started to do his observations from the Sun. Then he asked himself if that explained better what we see.

So Copernicus brought forward again the idea that the Earth and the other planets move round the Sun. You can feel what an exciting theory it was for him from his own words: "In the midst of all dwells the Sun . . . as if seated upon a royal throne the Sun rules the family of the planets as they circle round him."

This idea which had so pleased Copernicus also excited a German astronomer and mathematician called Johannes Kepler. But the idea still didn't fit what men saw – it left some things unexplained. Kepler spent many years trying to work out the shape of the path of the Earth and planets as they journeyed round the Sun. He made many calculations involving various curved paths; finally he could prove that the movement of the Earth and planets round the Sun was not circular but in the shape of an ellipse. "Ah, what a foolish bird I have been," Kepler is said to have remarked about those years he had spent.

Both Copernicus and Kepler have much in common with Columbus. All three had a great idea which filled their lives, and which contradicted what other people believed. For Columbus it was the idea of sailing west to Asia, for Copernicus it was the Sun at the centre of the Universe. In trying to prove their ideas, they discovered something new, something unexpected, which changed things even more than they had believed possible. Columbus died still thinking that he had discovered a route to Asia. It was left to other men to show that he had discovered a New World. In the same way, Kepler took on Copernicus' idea of an Earth that moved around the Sun, and worked out the shape of that movement, and found a new set of rules for the movement of the planets. Kepler was also particularly interested in the movements of our nearest neighbour in the sky, the Moon. He was the first to recognise that there was a connection between the movements of the Moon and movements of the tides in our oceans.

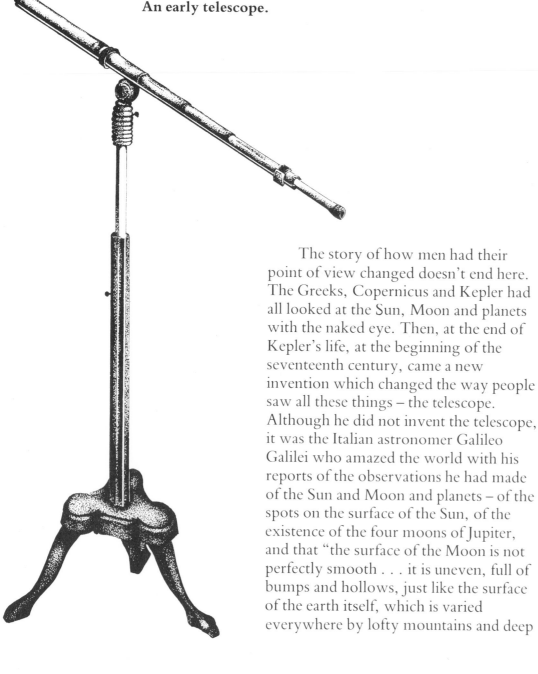

An early telescope.

The story of how men had their point of view changed doesn't end here. The Greeks, Copernicus and Kepler had all looked at the Sun, Moon and planets with the naked eye. Then, at the end of Kepler's life, at the beginning of the seventeenth century, came a new invention which changed the way people saw all these things – the telescope. Although he did not invent the telescope, it was the Italian astronomer Galileo Galilei who amazed the world with his reports of the observations he had made of the Sun and Moon and planets – of the spots on the surface of the Sun, of the existence of the four moons of Jupiter, and that "the surface of the Moon is not perfectly smooth . . . it is uneven, full of bumps and hollows, just like the surface of the earth itself, which is varied everywhere by lofty mountains and deep valleys." When Kepler heard of these discoveries he wrote to Galileo, and in that letter we can see him leaping ahead with thoughts of new discoveries which would be even greater than those of Columbus:

"There will be no lack of human pioneers when we have mastered the art of flight . . . Let us create vessels and sails adjusted to the heavens . . . There will be plenty of people unafraid of the empty wastes . . . In the meantime we shall prepare maps for the brave sky-travellers."

Kepler went further than dreaming of preparing maps. He wrote the first "science fiction" story which tells of man's first journey to the Moon. In his story the moon is a dreadful place with scorching hot days and frozen nights. Strange creatures live there in the underground caves during the long lunar day. While, at night, they come out to hunt. In his mind's eye, Kepler saw a sight that no human being was to see for over three hundred and fifty years. In his writing he imagined our planet Earth as seen from the lunar sky, with Africa looking like a human head cut off at the shoulders and Europe like a girl in a long robe bending down to kiss it.